I'm Afraid to Go Outside

Paul DiPietro

illustrations by
Jennifer Lenox

AUTHORS PLACE
—PRESS—

Published by Authors Place Press

9885 Wyecliff Drive, Suite 200

Highlands Ranch, CO 80126

Authorsplace.com

Manufactured in the United States of America.
ISBN: 978-1-62865-801-9

I would like to dedicate this book to my son Evan who brings me joy and happiness every day. His big heart, compassion for others, and thirst for knowledge gives me hope for the future.

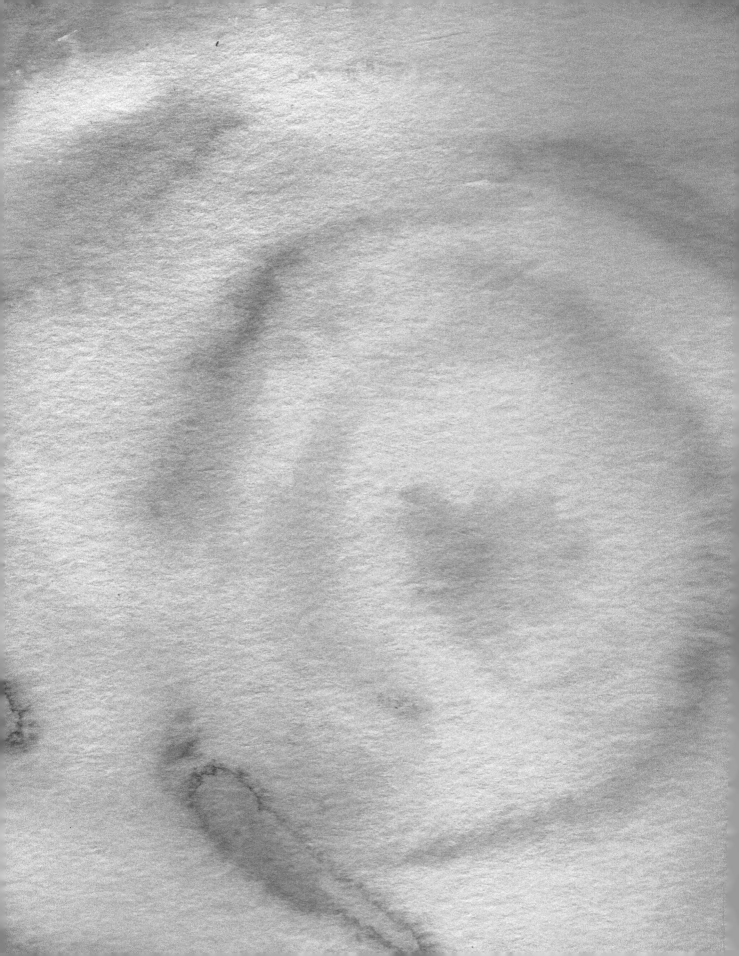

Barbara had always enjoyed playing outside, in her backyard, at the park and on the playground at shcool. Rain or shine, in all seasons. Barbara was happiest when she could be outdoors.

As winter came to an end, Barbara dreamt about warmer weather, bike rides, playdates with friends, trips to the park and long walks with her parents around her neighborhood.

Just as the snow melted and tiny buds began to appear on the trees outside her window, everything seemed to change.

Suddenly, everyone was talking about the Coronavirus and Covid-*19*. Barbara had heard those strange words on the television and the radio, over and over again. She wondered what they could mean.

"Barbara," her mother said one morning at breakfast time, "your school is closed for the rest of the week because there's a new virus that we do not want to catch. Dad and I will both be home too, because our work places are closed."

Follow up Questions:

1. When you hear the word Coronavirus, or
    Covid, what does this mean to you?

2. Since Covid, what are some things in your
    life that have changed, and how has these
    changesmade you feel?

3. How did it make you feel when your
    school was closed?

Barbara thought about this. She decided that the Coronavirus must be **very** bad and **very** scary, if the whole school was closed, and everyone had to stay home.

A week turned into a month, then two, then three. Barbara watched as her mother put on gloves and a mask to cover her face whenever she had to go out for groceries and other errands. Barbara missed seeing her friends. She hoped all of them were safe at home just like she was.

Follow up Questions:

1. Can you identify the safety equipment that Barbara saw her mother using in the story.

2. Why is it important to wear safety equipment when going into the community?

3. How does Barbara feel when she is thinking about her friends?
Is she happy, sad, mad, afraid?

4. How do you feel when you are not able to see and play with your friends?

"Barbara," her mother called to her one sunny morning. "It's a beautiful day. Let's go for a walk! Barbara was so excited to hear her mother suggest walking around the neighborhood. It had been weeks and weeks since Barbara had ventured beyond her yard. She ran to get her shoes, but then she remembered:

Covid-19

"Mom," she said, "is the virus gone?"

"Well, no," said her mother, "but I have a mask for you. It will keep you safe."

"and," said her father, noticing that Barbara looked a bit fearful, "I have a pair of gloves for you, to keep you extra safe!"

Barbara put on the mask and the gloves, just as her mother had done so many times before.

As soon as she stepped outside, she began to tremble. She looked around at the people walking on her sidewalk, and the cars coming and going, and she was overcome with fear. Barbara imagined the Coronavirus surrounding her and all of the other people outside.

Barbara
kicked off her
shoes and tore off
the gloves and mask as
she ran to her bedroom.

"No! I'm NOT going OUT," she cried.

Follow up Questions:

1. How is Barbara feeling about going outside in the community? Is she happy, sad, mad or afraid?

2. How do you feel about going out in the community during the Coronavirus pandemic?

Barbara's parents reassured her that it was okay to be afraid. Then they explained how wearing a mask and gloves would protect her from the virus.

"If a sick person touches a railing, and then you touch the railing with your gloves on, you won't get their germs. The gloves will keep the germs from touching your skin. If someone near you is sick, wearing a mask will keep you from breathing their germs into your mouth and nose."

Barbara's dad then showed Barbara a measuring tape and said, "If we work hard to stay six feet apart from other people," he pulled out the measuring tape to *1, 2, 3, 4, 5, 6* FEET, "we will be less likely to share any germs with them."
Barbara noticed that six feet was about the same length as her bed.

"The virus is not gone," dad said, "but if we take all of these precautions, we can safely go out into the community and stay healthy. Now, how about that walk?"

Barbara took a deep breath. When she looked out the window again, she noticed lots of other people wearing masks as they walked. She was glad that her parents had talked to her, and she liked the idea of staying safely within a six foot imaginary bubble, with her hands and face shielded from the virus.

Follow up Questions and Practice Session:

1. What are some things that we can do to be safe when going out in the community?

2. Practice what social distancing looks like. With a partner, measure out six feet.

Finally, Barbara put on her mask, her gloves and her shoes, and she stepped out into the warm fresh air. Armed with her safety equipment and a new understanding about what she could do to stay healthy, Barbara was feeling more confident about going out. With both of her parents at her side, she enjoyed a walk around the neighborhood.

THE END

About the Author

Paul DiPietro is a writer and Autism Specialist for the Holyoke MA Public School System. He has been working with individuals with Developmental Disabilities, Autism, and complex behavioral and emotional disabilities for the past 22 years.

Personally, Paul enjoys spending as much time with family and friends as possible, enjoys the ocean, music, cycling, swimming, and traveling. He enjoys sharing his knowledge and experience working with individuals with Autism to build awareness in the community. He believes that through knowledge and education you can inform change within the world.

Paul feels strongly that learning and education is the most important thing for our youth today. He believes in teaching our children not only to be successful but also to improve our world.

Find more about Paul DiPietro at growingupwithcourage.com or growingupwithcourage@gmail.com.

About the Illustrator

Jennifer Lenox is a Vermont artist and illustrator. She runs a custom artwork e-commerce business through Etsy.com, and is a featured artist at several Vermont fine art galleries. This is her first foray into the world of children's book illustration, though she has done technical illustrations for medical and physical therapy publications in the past. Jennifer spent several years teaching art at the elementary and middle level in both Vermont and New York state after earning her bachelors degree in studio art at Nazareth College, in Rochester, NY. Currently, she resides in Vermont with her husband and two young sons. You can find more of Jennifer's work at www.etsy.com/shop/JenniferLenoxVT.

9 781628 658019